ASTROLOGY

ARIES

BY TRUDY BECKER

Apex is distributed by North Star Editions:
sales@northstareditions.com | 888-417-0195

Produced for Apex by Red Line Editorial.

Photographs ©: Shutterstock Images, cover (illustration, constellation), cover (background), 1, 6, 9, 10–11, 12, 14–15, 16–17, 18, 20, 21, 22–23, 24, 26–27, 29; iStockphoto, 4–5, 7, 8; Dimitrios Kambouris/Getty Images for MTV/Paramount Global/Getty Images Entertainment/Getty Images, 25

Library of Congress Control Number: 2025939147

ISBN
979-8-89250-781-3 (hardcover)
979-8-89250-810-0 (paperback)
979-8-89250-867-4 (ebook pdf)
979-8-89250-839-1 (hosted ebook)

Printed in the United States of America
Mankato, MN
012026

NOTE TO PARENTS AND EDUCATORS

Apex books are designed to build literacy skills in striving readers. Exciting, high-interest content attracts and holds readers' attention. The text is carefully leveled to allow students to achieve success quickly. Additional features, such as bolded glossary words for difficult terms, help build comprehension.

TABLE OF CONTENTS

CHAPTER 1
THE RAM 4

CHAPTER 2
A STARRY CYCLE 10

CHAPTER 3
ABOUT ARIES 16

CHAPTER 4
A FIERY SIGN 22

COMPREHENSION QUESTIONS • 28
GLOSSARY • 30
TO LEARN MORE • 31
ABOUT THE AUTHOR • 31
INDEX • 32

CHAPTER 1

THE RAM

Aries is a **constellation** in the night sky. It has only a few main stars. They form a bent line.

A star chart is a map of the sky. It shows the shapes and locations of constellations.

In ancient Egypt, Aries was linked with the god Amun. He was sometimes shown with a ram's head.

Long ago, people thought this shape looked like a ram lying down. They named the constellation Aries. That means "ram" in Latin.

FAST FACT

The brightest star in Aries is called Hamal. That word is Arabic for "sheep."

Hamal is one of the stars that make up the ram's head.

A Greek **myth** linked Aries to a ram with golden wool. This ram saved a young man named Phrixus. Later, Phrixus offered the ram to the god Zeus. Zeus put the ram in the sky as a constellation.

Areas far from cities have darker skies. In these places, people can see more stars.

SOFT STARLIGHT

Aries is a small constellation. Also, its stars aren't very bright. So, it can be hard to see. To help, people can go out into the country on a night with no moonlight.

CHAPTER 2

A STARRY CYCLE

Aries is one of the **zodiac** signs. Each sign is matched with a constellation. Together, they form a cycle. It splits the year into 12 parts.

The zodiac is part of astrology, which claims that the movements of stars and planets shape people's lives.

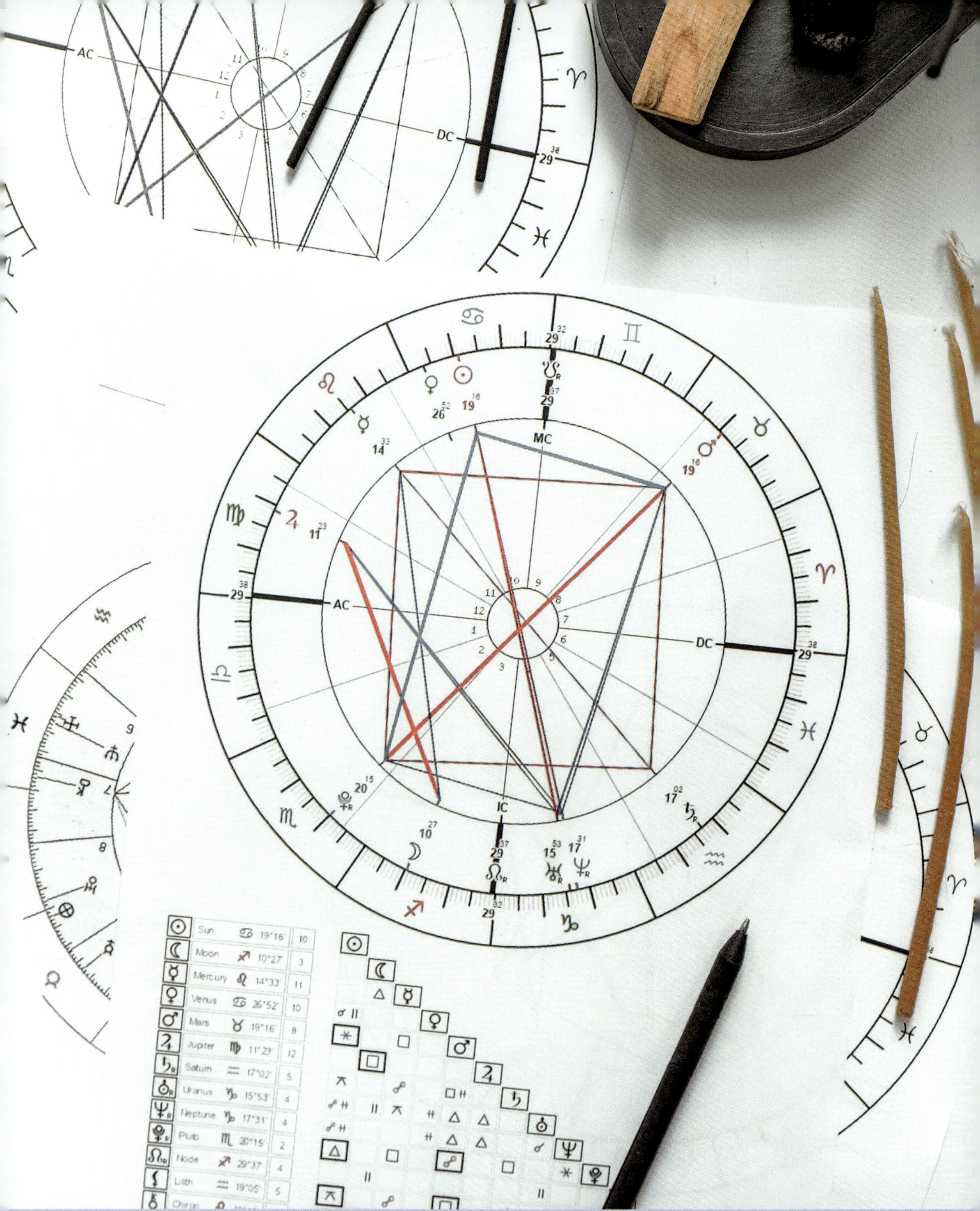
AC
DC
MC
IC
Sun ♋ 19°16' 10
Moon ♐ 10°27' 3
Mercury ♌ 14°33' 11
Venus ♋ 26°52' 10
Mars ♉ 19°16' 8
Jupiter ♍ 11°23' 12
Saturn ♒ 17°02' 5
Uranus ♑ 15°53' 4
Neptune ♑ 17°31' 4
Pluto ♏ 20°15' 2
Node ♐ 29°37' 4
Lilith ♒ 19°05' 5
Chiron

Aries is the first sign of the cycle. Its time starts around March 21. It lasts until about April 19. People born during this time have Aries as their **sun sign**.

FAST FACT

People have moon signs, too. Those are based on where the moon was when they were born.

A birth chart shows exactly where objects in space were when someone was born.

Some people believe their sun signs shape their **personalities**. For example, Aries is linked with being bold.

START OF SPRING

Aries begins when spring starts in northern parts of the world. As a result, Aries are said to be leaders. They may like to make change. Or they may be good at taking action.

Spring is when new plants begin to grow. It's a season of growth and change.

CHAPTER 3

ABOUT ARIES

The **glyph** for Aries looks like two curved lines. They connect at the bottom. The shape looks like a ram's horns.

A ram has large, curved horns on either side of its head.

Aries has fire as its **element**. People with fire signs are said to be brave. They may take risks. And they may have strong feelings.

SIMILAR SIGNS

In astrology, air signs and fire signs share some traits. People with these signs may think and act quickly. In contrast, people with earth signs may avoid change.

Fire is often a symbol of energy or power.

The planet Mars is a reddish color.

Aries's ruling planet is Mars. Astrology says ruling planets shape how people act. Mars is linked with energy and action.

FAST FACT

Mars is named after the Roman god of war.

In Roman myths, the god Mars was a strong fighter.

CHAPTER 4

A FIERY SIGN

Aries are said to be **passionate**. They may have strong likes and dislikes. They often care deeply about their family and friends.

Aries may like trying new things and getting together with friends.

Playing sports can be a good way for Aries to shine. They often work hard to be the best.

Aries may be competitive, too. They may like to win. And they may work hard to reach their goals.

FAST FACT

Famous Aries include Lady Gaga and Emma Watson. Lisa from BLACKPINK is an Aries, too.

Lisa and BLACKPINK have won many music awards.

Aries are also known for being honest. They say what they think. Sometimes, this can hurt people's feelings. But it also makes Aries good friends.

PROS AND CONS

A sign's traits can be good or bad. Aries may speak or act without thinking. They may get mad quickly. But they are also quick to forgive. And they protect people they love.

Rams are known for butting heads. Aries may also tend to get into fights.

COMPREHENSION QUESTIONS

Write your answers on a separate piece of paper.

1. Write a few sentences describing the traits an Aries is said to have.

2. Do you like taking risks? Why or why not?

3. Which element is Aries matched with?

- **A.** air
- **B.** fire
- **C.** water

4. Why would being honest make Aries good friends?

- **A.** Their friends can trust them to tell the truth.
- **B.** They will only say nice things to their friends.
- **C.** Good friends never feel angry.

5. What does **traits** mean in this book?

*In astrology, air signs and fire signs share some **traits**. People with these signs may think and act quickly.*

- **A.** times of day
- **B.** ways of acting
- **C.** types of food

6. What does **competitive** mean in this book?

*Aries may be **competitive**, too. They may like to win.*

- **A.** wanting to sit back and watch
- **B.** wanting to be the best
- **C.** wanting to share with others

Answer key on page 32.

GLOSSARY

constellation

A group of stars that form a shape.

element

One of four forces (air, earth, fire, or water) that each zodiac sign is matched with and said to be shaped by.

glyph

A shape that stands for a word or idea.

myth

A well-known story from the past that often includes magic.

passionate

Having strong feelings or beliefs.

personalities

How people usually act.

sun sign

A person's main zodiac sign, which is decided by the date they were born.

zodiac

The set of 12 signs used in astrology, based on a part of the sky that the sun appears to move through each year.

TO LEARN MORE

BOOKS

Goldstein, Margaret J. *Mysteries of Stars*. Lerner Publications, 2021.

Ha, Christine. *Zeus*. Apex Editions, 2022.

McMullen, Gemma. *The Stars*. Little Blue House, 2025.

ONLINE RESOURCES

Visit **www.apexeditions.com** to find links and resources related to this title.

ABOUT THE AUTHOR

Trudy Becker lives in Minneapolis, Minnesota. Her sun sign is Aries. She likes books and exploring new places.

INDEX

B
bold, 14

C
competitive, 24
constellation, 4, 6, 8–9, 10

E
element, 19

F
famous Aries, 25
fire signs, 19

G
glyph, 16

H
Hamal, 7
honest, 26

M
Mars, 20–21
moon signs, 13

P
passionate, 22
Phrixus, 8

R
ram, 6, 8, 16
ruling planet, 20

S
spring, 14
sun signs, 13–14

Z
Zeus, 8
zodiac, 10

ANSWER KEY:
1. Answers will vary; 2. Answers will vary; 3. B; 4. A; 5. B; 6. B